P9-CRQ-408

Shenandoah

NATIONAL PARK

impressions

photography by

Pat and Chuck Blackley

FARCOUNTRY
PRESS

Right: *Pink blossoms in the foreground point toward the park's repeating ridges. It's no wonder these mountains were named the "blue ridge."*

Title page: *The gently rounded hills and slopes of Shenandoah are outlined with the colors of foliage in spring, summer, and fall.*

Front cover: *Fog is a frequent visitor to Shenandoah. Here it settles along the Appalachian Trail and snuggles up to the luxurious blooms of mountain laurel.*

Back cover: *In summertime, waterfalls such as Jones River Falls can seem like oases to hot, tired hikers.*

ISBN: 1-56037-230-3
Photographs © Pat and Chuck Blackley
© 2003 Farcountry Press

Captions by Karen Michaud, Patressa Smelser, and Joanne Amberson

This book may not be reproduced in whole or in part by any means (with the exception of short quotes for the purpose of review) without the permission of the publisher.
For more information on our books write: Farcountry Press, P.O. Box 5630, Helena, MT 59604 or call (800) 654-1105 or visit www.montanamagazine.com

Created, produced, and designed in the United States.
Printed in China.

Above: *Trumpet honeysuckle is one of the park's easier wildflowers to spot. Who could miss this bright scarlet bloom?*

Facing page: *Mountain laurel blooms along a Shenandoah trail near Blackrock.*

FOREWORD

by Claire Comer,
Shenandoah National Park Interpretive Specialist

Not far from the madding crowd, just west of the nation's capital, is an oasis of nature, Shenandoah National Park. Here, the rolling piedmont of Virginia suddenly stretches up to reach the sky and the ancient ridges of the Blue Ridge Mountains beckon, promising tranquillity and renewal.

On each ridge and in each hollow lies a story, an interwoven tale of humans and nature and the never-ending quest to live in harmony. Swift mountain streams tumble down the draws, carrying life to those within and beyond Shenandoah's boundary. A birdsong symphony rides the morning breeze, serenading the sanctuary of migratory birds. Acres of wilderness, home to wildlife, belie the former attempts to conquer this rugged mountain terrain for commercial use. And in these stories lies Shenandoah's past as well as its future.

Shenandoah National Park's beauty offers refuge to millions of visitors each year. Skyline Drive, the only public road into the park, winds along the crest of the Blue Ridge, rewarding motorists with views of the rolling hills of the piedmont to the east and a horizon of peaks and valleys to the west. Five hundred miles of trails take hikers into the world of the forest, a chance to discover the denizens of nature: white-tailed deer, black bears, tiny chipmunks, and more. Mimicking the path of Skyline Drive, the Appalachian Trail is a "wilderness way through civilization" for adventurers making the trek from Georgia to Maine. This footpath covers more than 2,000 miles and 101 of them are in the park. Rapidan Camp, Skyland Resort, and countless remnants of the Civilian Conservation Corps provide the backdrop for Shenandoah's historic allure. Visitors can experience the Blue Ridge of the past at Rapidan Camp, President and Mrs. Herbert Hoover's "summer White House," or revisit the "Roaring '20s" at Skyland Resort.

Shenandoah National Park boasts several varieties of wild violets, including the bird's-foot violet, named for the shape of its leaf.

As European settlers headed west, the Blue Ridge Mountains were the first they encountered. They found abundant wildlife and lush hardwood forests. Just across the ancient worn-down ridges they found the fertile Shenandoah Valley, its rich, dark soil a Mecca to farmers. Like the Native Americans before them, many recognized the tremendous value of the

resources of the mountains and valley and settled in to make a life for themselves.

Valley farmers began producing crops, and as the eastern population grew so did the demand for the farmers' harvests. Transporting those goods proved challenging until the railroad began its journey west. The boom for agricultural products was soon matched by the demand for timber to be used for railroad ties. More and more people moved to the mountains, cultivating small patches of ground, planting orchards, and harvesting a variety of timber products. Valley farmers began acquiring large tracts of land for grazing while timber and mining companies bought up logging and mineral rights. As in much of the East, the abundant wildlife and lush hardwood forests were becoming casualties of progress.

Entrepreneurs jumped in on the land-grab to develop fashionable resorts for vacationing urbanites. Blackrock Springs and Skyland Resort touted superior air and water and fought to retain some of the beauty of the mountains amidst the work of the timber companies. Tourism became a viable industry for Virginia residents. As post–Civil War economics evolved, valley businessmen looked for ways to develop tourism in hopes of preserving the state's scenic beauty while maintaining its economic quality of life.

The businessmen were ecstatic when they learned of the National Park Service's search for suitable land to establish an eastern national park. They quickly joined the crusade vying for attention for a Virginia park. Their efforts were rewarded when, in 1926, Congress authorized a national park to be located in the Blue Ridge Mountains of Virginia. Virginia's park supporters campaigned to raise the money necessary to buy the land within the proposed boundary. Meanwhile, many landowners and residents balked at the idea of losing their land and homes.

Ten years, several lawsuits, two boundary reductions, and a blanket condemnation later, Virginia presented the federal government with a deed for more than 160,000 acres, and

Shenandoah National Park was established. The new park comprised more than a thousand previously privately owned tracts. Nearly 500 families were displaced, their abandoned homes dotting the landscape. Hillsides lay nearly barren, the result of the timber companies' last ditch effort to extract valuable lumber. The task of making this an eastern park "in the western mold" must have seemed daunting. Almost immediately help arrived in the form of Franklin Roosevelt's Tree Army, the Civilian Conservation Corps (CCC), a Depression-era work relief program.

Over the next nine years thousands of young CCC men toiled in the mountains of Virginia constructing trails and

A hiker is rewarded with a view toward 4,010-foot Stony Man Mountain, one of Virginia's highest peaks.

facilities, planting trees and shrubs—building a national park. Mother Nature did her part as well, welcoming home native plants and animals. Rangers arrived to plan management, patrol Skyline Drive, and assist the throngs of visitors flocking to the park. Facilities opened, plants and trees grew, and animals settled in to make a home for themselves. Once again explorers encountered lush hardwood forests and abundant wildlife. But now the explorers were naturalists and hikers, and the forests and wildlife were protected. Full circle? Not in the world of nature.

Nature evolves, changing from decade to decade, reflecting

the changing universe—sometimes better, sometimes not, but always different. The Shenandoah you encounter today is a dynamic environment and every visitor becomes part of the continuum. As you enter the animals' home you leave behind the conventions of civilization. You have the opportunity to observe wildlife in its natural habitat, to see what plants thrive naturally in a variety of soils, elevations, and exposures, to experience the views from the mountaintop.

The animals that find protection among the forested ridges of Shenandoah include more than 50 mammal species, 51 reptile and amphibian species, 30 fish species, and more than 200

The lithe flowers of black cohosh rise elegantly above the forest floor.

resident and transient bird species—and those are just the ones we know about! Providing the most diverse habitat in the park is its centerpiece, Big Meadows. This 130-acre meadow is an historic landscape. Evidence indicates that it has been maintained since before the arrival of European settlers. When or why it was created is unclear, but its open areas have hosted Native American hunters, farms, a CCC camp, a presidential dedication, World War II training squads, and now, the majority of the park's rare and endangered plants. At the center of the meadow is an unexpected wetland adding to its intrigue. Animals of all species are attracted to the intermittent swamp, making it a favorite spot among wildlife observers.

Perhaps the most visible of Shenandoah's residents are the white-tailed deer. Thousands of these graceful creatures inhabit the park, frequenting developed areas for their favored vegetation. Deer browse the edge along Skyline Drive because tender saplings thrive there. Careful observers will notice the "browse line"—the line below which deer have stripped all leaves and twigs. Because deer are drawn to the area along the Drive, motorists must be extra careful. Many deer-vehicle accidents happen in Shenandoah each year.

In late spring, white-tailed fawns are born. For their first few weeks of life they hide silently in grassy areas like Big Meadows while their mothers browse. Their signature spots offer camouflage. As an added defense, they are born scentless. During those first crucial days mothers will return only for nursing so their own scent doesn't attract predators.

The intense sunlight of the spring triggers a hormone in male deer that stimulates the growth of their antlers. During this growth phase the antlers are distinguished by a velvety covering that contains blood vessels to nourish the rapidly growing antlers. Early in the fall the deer will use saplings to rub the covering from their antlers in preparation for mating or "rutting" season. During rut, deer can be especially unpredictable and even dangerous, another reason for visitors to keep their distance.

The common names of Shenandoah's many wildflowers are fun to learn and know, and range from sturdy and practical "horse nettle" (foreground) to whimsical "butter and eggs" (background).

The meadow and edge areas attract other species as well. Groundhogs perch along the roadside munching warily, poised to flee to the safety of their burrow if necessary. Chipmunks and squirrels may make a mad dash across the road, and occasionally Shenandoah's less brazen residents can be seen; bobcats, wild turkeys, foxes, and bears are more accustomed to the deeper forest areas.

Equally shy, but more visible and vocal, are the birds of Shenandoah National Park. Here again, the meadow and edge areas create places for nesting and feeding as well as accessible places for visitors to observe. The bright-blue indigo bunting is an eye-catcher, as is the American goldfinch. These flashes of color are accompanied by the "sweet-sweet, chew-chew, sweet-sweet" and "potato CHIP, potato CHIP, potato CHIP" songs of these two common birds. Rose-breasted grosbeak and ruffed grouse entice avid bird-watchers deep into the forest where these species make their homes.

Several species of hawks and owls live and hunt in Shenandoah. These birds of prey contribute to nature's balance, scooping up mice, moles, chipmunks, and snakes. Other species feed on Shenandoah's aquatic life. The Louisiana water thrush builds its nest along stream banks and shares the mayflies with trout.

Food and shelter for this array of wildlife are provided by Shenandoah's plant life, which is as varied as its inhabitants. Plants, too, are habitat sensitive, some preferring the open areas of meadow and edge, while others thrive in the cool shade of the forest. As any gardener knows, the most vibrant color is supplied by sun-loving flowers. Bright Deptford pinks, golden lilies, and black-eyed Susans along Skyline Drive delight motorists. But the rewards for the deep-woods hiker are no less: translucent Indian pipes and great expanses of ferns thrive under the canopy of both deciduous and evergreen trees. Perhaps the greatest color show of Shenandoah is supplied by the trees themselves. A monochromatic yet lush green through the summer, these same trees produce riotous color when their leaves respond to the cooler temperatures of fall.

Shenandoah has a mixture of deciduous hardwood and evergreen trees. Because of the varied elevations in the park, ranging from 1,000 to 4,000 feet, in addition to the usual Virginia trees, Shenandoah has an occasional balsam fir or red spruce commonly found in the cooler north. Oaks are predominant and include red, white, and chestnut. Poplar, hickory, and maple are also common. Among evergreens, white, pitch, scrub, and table mountain pines lend a bit of color to the winter season. Some hemlock can still be found. These cathedral-like trees with flat needles are among Shenandoah's oldest trees, some older than 500 years, but the entire species is rapidly succumbing to the hemlock woolly adelgid, an aphid that literally sucks the life from eastern hemlocks.

The loss of the hemlocks is a tragedy, but the forest will endure and compensate, just as it did after the American chestnut blight stole that once dominant tree from the landscape, leaving only its struggling roots and saplings. Insects, blight, invasive plants, and acid rain, as well as ice, wind, and drought all take their toll on the forest. The role of many National Park Service rangers has become that of scientist, studying, monitoring, and managing for the future. In Shenandoah, botanists work to control invasive species that threaten native plants. Biologists study changes in water and the resulting changes in wildlife and plant life. Air quality specialists monitor pollution. Cultural resource specialists stabilize, restore, and protect the park's special places and objects. From their work, the stories of Shenandoah's past and its hope for the future emerge.

As Shenandoah's care passes from generation to generation, new challenges come to light. However, the one constant is the park's ability to renew and delight each generation of visitors. In the 1930s families arrived, their cars packed full of camping gear and picnic supplies. They hiked to tumbling waterfalls and climbed to spectacular vistas. They roasted marshmallows in the campgrounds and slept under the stars. Today, their children and grandchildren still arrive with full cars and great expectations.

Shenandoah never fails them. Six wonderful waterfalls still tumble through Whiteoak Canyon, and Hawksbill Peak is still the window to forever. A sea of morning fog severs the mountaintop, then lifts to reveal the valley below. Each sunrise and sunset paints meadows and ridges bright orange and deep purple. Wildflowers bloom and the leaves change color. The animals prepare for the winter and children pick blueberries in the meadow. And the old becomes new for each generation.

Shenandoah National Park: immerse yourself in its beauty, its past, its present, and its future. ✧

Shenandoah boasts a happy abundance of gurgling mountain streams, such as Hogcamp Branch.

Above: The white-tailed deer so abundant in Shenandoah are responsible for some of the park's prettiest scenes.

Facing page: Watching the sun set from a west-facing overlook along Skyline Drive is understandably popular among park visitors.

Above: *Skyland is a fine place to savor a sunset.*

Facing page: *The town of Waynesboro, Virginia, settles in for the night.*

Above: *As seen from Browntown Overlook, fog makes the valley below seem almost like a dream.*

Facing page: *Explore the "Roaring '20s" at historic Skyland Resort.*

Above: *Water drapes like chiffon over rock at South River Falls.*

Facing page: *The delightful surprises of Shenandoah's forests include opulent blooming wildflowers like Turk's-cap lilies and black cohosh.*

Above: *"Who goes there?" a white-tailed deer fawn seems to ask.*

Facing page: *The colors and light of a sunset over Shenandoah Valley can seem almost unreal, even spooky—but always beautiful.*

Above: *Trillium is one of the park's "signature" spring wildflowers. The trillium flower is white when new and becomes a lovely deep pink as it ages.*

Right: *Mountain laurel beckons the viewer's eye to a collage of Shenandoah's ethereal, almost mystical-looking ridges.*

Above: *Autumn bathes Shenandoah's forests in fiery gold.*

Facing page: *A single sunbeam spotlights one tree-covered Shenandoah mountaintop. The Appalachian Mountains, of which Shenandoah is a part, are old and worn down to a series of softly sloping hills and hollows.*

Above: *Mountain laurel blooms to perfection along the Appalachian Trail at Sawmill Ridge.*

Facing page: *Black bears in Shenandoah feed on fruit, nuts, and berries, along with some insects.*
For this black bear, an apple is a convenient snack.

Above: *The first leaves of spring in Shenandoah are green and gold and lovely.*

Facing page: *Waterfalls often create sculptures of stunning beauty in winter. Dark Hollow Falls is shown here at work.*

Above: Dyer's woad blooms lemon yellow along Skyline Drive.

Right: Bloodroot is one of the very first wildflowers of spring in the park.

Facing page: To see most of the park's waterfalls some hiking is required, but the rewards are great. Doyles River Falls is a graceful, pretty example.

Early autumn near Loft Mountain shows a first splash of gold and promises more vivid colors in the weeks to come.

The Blue Ridge Mountains can seem like so many layers of tissue paper in the early or late hours of the day.

Above: *Hikers enjoy the snow on the Dark Hollow Falls Trail.*

Right: *Looking west from a high point: a forested ridge, a valley, and Massanutten Mountain beyond. Winter visitors might feel as if the park's snow-covered rocks, quiet trails, and parfait sunsets are all theirs, since park visitation is lowest then.*

Right: *Spiderwort is a deep-purple Shenandoah wildflower.*

Below: *Fly poison blooms in Big Meadows.*

Facing page: *Views from overlooks in the summer offer a panoply of greens and textures.*

Above: *Skyline Drive curves along the park's spine, providing a pleasant and unhurried way to experience Shenandoah.*

Left: *A fringe of golden grasses lines a view from Skyline Drive near the park's north entrance.*

Above: *Milkweed—a preferred food for the monarch butterfly— blooms in a park meadow in the summer.*

Facing page: *Visitors take in the view at The Point Overlook.*

Above: *Deptford pink is one of Shenandoah's vibrantly colored summer wildflowers.*

Facing page: *Shenandoah's streams—like this one, the Laurel Prong fork of the Rapidan River—are enjoyed by fishermen and hikers alike.*

Above: *This young black bear is one of perhaps 300 in the park.*

Facing page: *Rapidan Camp, "summer White House" of President Herbert and First Lady Lou Henry Hoover (1929–1933), is a National Historic Landmark and favorite destination of park visitors.*

The sun rises and the sun sets—and Shenandoah turns to gold.

Above: Delicately colored mushrooms colonize a fallen tree.

Left: Visitors delight in seeing white-tailed deer in Big Meadows, the largest open area in the park.

Above: *Yellow lady's-slippers grow in the park, a not-so-common visual treat for lucky hikers.*

Facing page: *Springtime's bright green glows through the fog.*

Above: *From one Appalachian Trail hiker to another, some friendly advice. On Sawmill Ridge.*

Left: *Fog makes the park's visitors look more closely—at lichen-covered rocks, at trees, at blossoms.*

Above: *Some visitors have prime seats for a sunset over the Shenandoah Valley.*

Facing page: *A waterfall offers chilly refreshment on the Whiteoak Canyon Trail.*

Left: *Puffs of fog dot the view east to the Charlottesville Reservoir.*

Below: *Mountain laurel begins to bloom above a carpet of ferns.*

Right: *The gorgeous Turk's-cap lily is not one of Shenandoah's most frequently seen wildflowers, but it is certainly one of its most spectacular.*

Below: *Chickweed is a dainty and common member of the park's wildflower lineup.*

Facing page: *Waterfalls such as Jones River Falls provide visual sustenance for hikers.*

Above: *Big Meadows is home to many different wildflowers, though in this photo the ox-eye daisy appears to be solely on display.*

Facing page: *A mushroom masterpiece called "hen-of-the-woods" grows at the base of a tree, ready to delight hikers.*

Massanutten Mountain, capped by sandstone, stands above more easily eroded limestone formations, and splits the Shenandoah Valley in half for 50 miles of its length.

Above: *All summer the common milkweed with its lavender blooms stands tall.*

Left: *One narrow view: rocks, trees, and a far mountain ridge.*

Above: *Caught out of forest shadows, a fawn's camouflage fails.*

Facing page: *Native Americans may have used fire to clear areas like Big Meadows for hunting and berry-producing shrubs.*

Above: *Blue-eyed grass is a delightfully named and sprightly park wildflower.*

Left: *Trees produce every lush shade of green imaginable in a forest area near Sawmill Run.*

Facing page: *The moon rises over Moormans River, creating a cool purple scene.*

Above: *These deer may be at play or coveting a particularly tasty patch of vegetation.*

Facing page: *Bicycling along Skyline Drive is a wonderful way to experience Shenandoah. Like automobile drivers, cyclists should observe the 35-mile-per-hour speed limit.*

End of day paints the Shenandoah sky and everything below it with stunning fiery shades.

Purple coneflowers attract a monarch butterfly.

At Milam Gap, apple blossoms and a traditional fence are reminders of the families who once lived here.

Spectacular beams of sunlight shine over the Shenandoah Valley.

Above: *Mountain laurel blooms are like tiny pink and red teacups.*

Left: *Stony Man Overlook offers a first-rate, easy way to see 4,010-foot Stony Man Mountain. Can you see the "man" for which the mountain is named?*

Above: *Corbin Cabin is reminiscent of some of the more rustic homes of the former mountain residents. It is maintained as a rental cabin by the Potomac Appalachian Trail Club.*

Facing page: *Patches of fog lift on a summer day in Shenandoah.*

Above: *This white-tailed deer mama and her two fawns are part of the large deer population in Shenandoah National Park.*

Facing page: *Autumn in the park is a palette of every conceivable warm color.*

Above: *A swallowtail butterfly feeds on the nectar of wild bergamot, a member of the mint family.*

Left: *Opportunistic hunters, raccoons adapt to whatever food sources become available. This raccoon investigates a bear-proof trash receptacle.*

Facing page: *A Shenandoah hiker pauses for the long view on Stony Man Mountain.*

Pat and Chuck Blackley are a photographic and writing team who work throughout North America. With a love of the outdoors and of the Blue Ridge Mountains in particular, they find Shenandoah National Park to be a favorite subject.

Their work appears in numerous magazines including *Backpacker*, *Blue Ridge Country*, *Country*, *Family Fun*, *Outdoor America*, and *Travel Holiday*, and in books by such publishers as Falcon, Farcountry Press, IDG Books (Frommer's), Insight Guides, Leisure Publishing, Lerner, National Geographic, Ulysses Press, and Walking Stick Press. Additionally, American Park Network, Forbes Special Interest, Impact Photographics, KC Publications, Virginia Tourism Corporation, and The Wilderness Society publish the Blackleys in calendars and commercial projects.